Acknowledgements

Thanks!

This journal would not be possible without the creativity and commitment of a whole network of change agents, activists, entrepreneurs and mavericks.

I would like to thank ALL of those who've been involved in this BusinessPath journey.

In particular, thanks to Mike Henson for providing some of your excellent illustration work and Melanie Ray for your help with aspects of the design process.

Thanks also to Tom Slater, Ben Taylor and all at Newforms for the work you've done on this journal and your commitment to creativity, innovation and pioneering new forms that are changing the world!

Peter J Farmer

First published in Great Britain in 2017 by
The Book Guild Ltd
9 Priory Business Park
Wistow Road, Kibworth
Leicestershire, LE8 0RX
Freephone: 0800 999 2982
www.bookguild.co.uk
Email: info@bookguild.co.uk
Twitter: @bookguild

Newforms Business Journal
www.newformsbusiness.com
Copyright © 2017 Peter J Farmer

The right of Peter J Farmer to be identified as the author of this
work has been asserted by him in accordance with the
Copyright, Design and Patents Act 1988.

Sources of quotes for entrepreneur stories:

Jamal Edwards: www.theguardian.com/small-business-network/2016/apr/08/jamal-edwards-
sbtv-youtube-business-money-passion

Pip Murray: www.startups.co.uk/inspiring-women-pip-murray/,
http://startups.co.uk/top-new-businesses-of-2015-pip-nut/ and www.startups.co.uk/the-start-
up-shed-why-it-pays-to-get-creative-when-looking-for-start-up-investment

Rita Sharma: www.tenentrepreneurs.org/author/rita-sharma

Printed and bound in Great Britain by CPI Group (UK) Ltd, Croydon, CR0 4YY

ISBN 978 1912083 534

British Library Cataloguing in Publication Data.
A catalogue record for this book is available from the British Library

newforms

BUSINESS PATH JOURNAL

A CREATIVE START-UP PLANNER!

WELCOME...

...to your business start-up journey!

Let's get going....

This book is to...

Write in it...

Dream in it!

Scribble in it...

Draw in it...

ENJOY!

CONTENTS

Money matters
& Legal Stuff!

Finding your
key clients

7.
MULTIPLY

6.
PLAY

5.
KEY

4.
WHEEL

Who are your
customers?

Define your
customer's
experience

The lifestyle of
an Entrepreneur

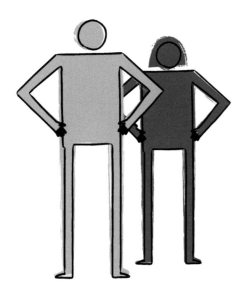

What does it mean to be an Entrepreneur?

How can you think and act like an Entrepreneur?

"Rather than working as an employee, an entrepreneur runs a business and assumes all the risk and reward of a given business venture, idea, good or service offered for sale. The entrepreneur is commonly seen as a business leader and innovator of new ideas and business processes."

(www.investopedia.com)

An entrepreneur has been defined as "a person who organizes and manages any enterprise, especially a business, usually with considerable initiative and risk."

(Dictionary.com)

Introduction:
ENTREPRENEURS

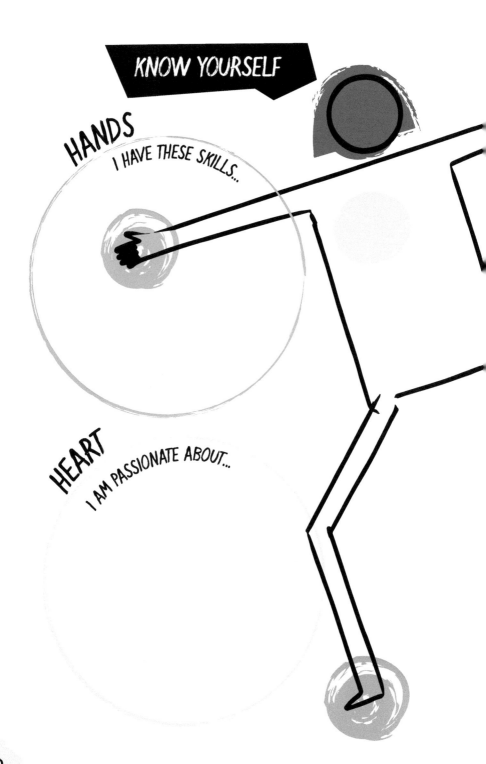

KNOW YOURSELF

HANDS

I HAVE THESE SKILLS...

HEART

I AM PASSIONATE ABOUT...

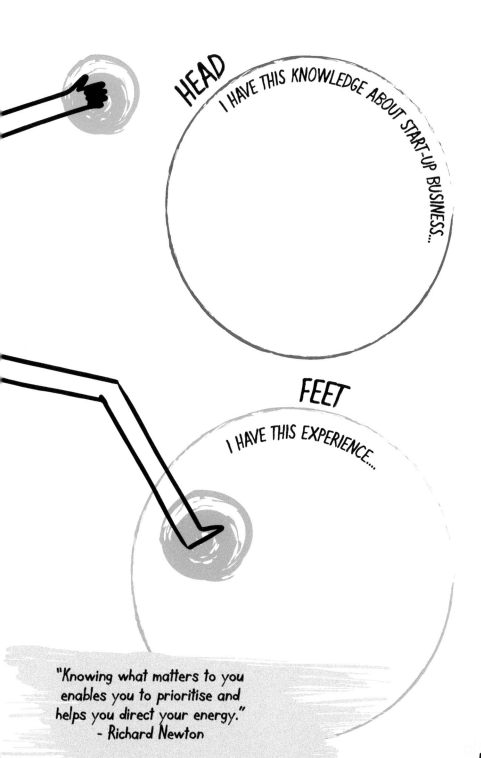

HEAD

I HAVE THIS KNOWLEDGE ABOUT START-UP BUSINESS...

FEET

I HAVE THIS EXPERIENCE....

"Knowing what matters to you enables you to prioritise and helps you direct your energy."
- Richard Newton

STOP

Use this opportunity to really stop and
think about what lies ahead!

TOP TIPS TO HELP YOU STOP AND THINK:
- Turn off your laptop, phone, tablet!
- Go for walks
- Do something creative
- Change Location

3

TIMES STEVEN SPIELBERG WAS REJECTED
BY THE UNIVERSITY OF SOUTHERN
CALIFORNIA, THEN HE DROPPED OUT
TO BECOME A DIRECTOR

What feelings/thoughts come to mind when you consider the start-up Journey ahead...

WRITE HERE...

G T
RE DY

What do you need to do to
prepare yourself to start up?

"If I have nine hours to chop
down a tree I'd spend the first
six hours sharpening my axe."
- Abraham Lincoln

WRITE HERE...

GO

What are your top 5 priorities
to go and do immediately?

"The ones who are crazy
enough to think that they can
change the world are the
ones who do." - Steve Jobs

WRITE HERE...

My STRENGTHS are...

"In a world that is changing really quickly, the only strategy that is guaranteed to fail is not taking risks."
- Mark Zuckerberg

My WEAKNESSES are...

YOUR TIME

"Nothing comes by merely
thinking about it."
- John Wanamaker

	MONDAY	TUESDAY	WEDNESDAY
MORNING			
AFTERNOON			
EVENING			

20

What are your current time commitments?
Fill them in below.
When will you make time to work on your business?
Guard this time with your life!

THURSDAY	FRIDAY	SATURDAY	SUNDAY

Picture your future business.

Plan your journey...

1. PICTURE

Steve Jobs

"We started out to get
a computer in the hands
of everyday people, and
we succeeded beyond
our wildest dreams."

In 1975, the 20-year-old Jobs and Wozniak set up shop in Jobs' parents' garage, dubbed the venture 'Apple', and began working on the prototype of the Apple I. To generate the $1,350 in capital they used to start Apple, Steve Jobs sold his Volkswagen microbus, and Steve Wozniak sold his Hewlett-Packard calculator. Although the Apple I sold mainly to hobbyists, it generated enough cash to enable Jobs and Wozniak to improve and refine their design. Much of Jobs' time was spent working his kitchen, where he spent hours on the phone trying to find investors for the company.

In 1977 they introduced the Apple II - the first personal computer with colour graphics and a keyboard. Designed for beginners the user-friendly Apple II was a tremendous success, ushering in the era of the personal computer. First-year sales topped $3 million. Two years later, sales ballooned to $200 million.

In 1979, after a tour of PARC (Palo Alto Research Center Incorporated), Jobs saw the commercial potential of the Xerox Alto, which was mouse-driven and had a graphical user interface. This led to development of the unsuccessful Apple Lisa in 1983, followed by the breakthrough Macintosh in 1984.

Notes:
(what stood out, what was inspiring, or encouraging??

WHICH IDEA?

Use the space in the houses to write down your many business ideas...

My most exciting idea...

The idea that I think most matches my skills...

My most profitable idea...

"Chase the vision, not the money, the money will end up following you."
- Tony Hsieh

My most unique idea...

Other ideas...

The idea that I am taking forward is...

27

PICTURE YOUR FUTURE

1. Put on some relaxing music

2. Close your eyes and relax

3. Picture 10 years in the future

✿ What do you see yourself doing?
✿ What do you have?
✿ What will you be?

Spend some time exploring what you see or hear.

4. Write down the key things you visualised in the house...

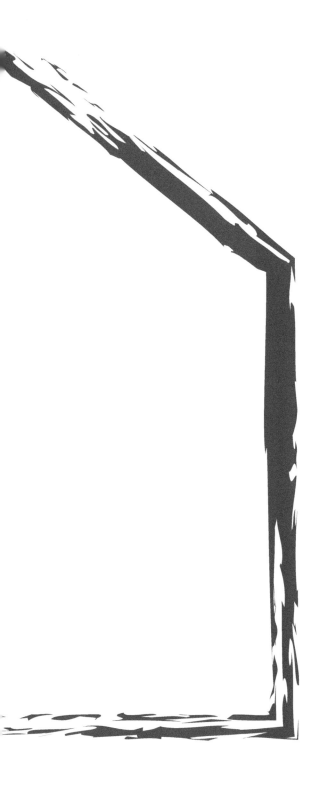

FUTURE GOALS

What do you see yourself having, being and doing in 5 years time?

I HAVE...

I AM...

I AM DOING...

5 years time

FUTURE GOALS

What do you see yourself having, being and doing in 1 years time?

I HAVE...

I AM...

I AM DOING...

1 years time

YOUR BUSINESS NAME

Use the clouds below to write your potential business name ideas. keep in mind that the name should be easy to remember and it should help people understand what you offer, as well as being creative...

BUSINESS NAME
(WRITE YOUR FINAL
IDEA HERE)

WORLD-CHANGING IDEAS...

How can your ideas change the world?
Use the clouds to write your world-changing ideas.

"Let's go invent tomorrow instead of worrying about what happened yesterday."
- Steve Jobs

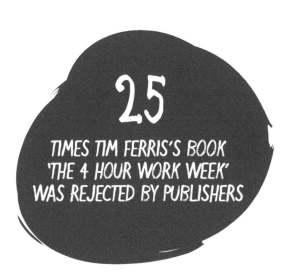

25

TIMES TIM FERRIS'S BOOK
'THE 4 HOUR WORK WEEK'
WAS REJECTED BY PUBLISHERS

WE EXIST TO...

Finish this sentence inside
the earth below.

My business exists to...

LAUNCH TIMELINE

Write on the timeline what you
need to do and when before you
launch your enterprise.

TODAY

When will you launch
your enterprise?

LAUNCH
DATE

Map your potential customers...

2. MAP

Justine Roberts

Justine and her colleagues didn't receive a penny from their website for five years - a hardship she dubbed a blessing in disguise...

Justine has been voted the seventh most powerful woman in the UK by BBC's Woman's Hour, a programme that offers a womans prospective on the world. She Is often referred to as one of the best female enterpreneurs in Britain. She is the co-founder of Mumsnet and it's CEO for 16 years. Mumsnet is the biggest network for working parents that boasts seven million visits and 50 million page views monthly. It preceded Facebook and Twitter.

Justine and her entrepreneurial journey began after she became pregnant and quit her job at an English bank. She had decided to focus on motherhood rather than a job where she thought there was no time for family. Her business idea was conceived during that period, at which she describes a "Eureka moment."

The start-up was a challenge for Justine. With dot com bubble bursting, timing was against her and for five whole years Justine and her colleagues didn't receive a penny from the website. They had to grow it organically, a hardship she dubbed a blessing in disguise, that showed her their business model was not sustainable.

The obstacles however, were not only strictly logistical. Justine was a victim of cyber-harassment and bullying that was taken to the next level when a SWAT unit surrounded her house after receiving a tip about a hostage situation or when the user accounts of her website were hacked into and otherwise compromised.

Despite all that, she claims the hardship and obstacles made her more tough and resilient and resulted in not only creating one of the most successful websites around, but also inspiring an entire movement for working parents.

Notes:

CUSTOMER PROFILE 1

Think about 4 different types of customers you could have. Write on the following pages...

NAME OF CUSTOMER PROFILE:
(e.g. Mums with kids)

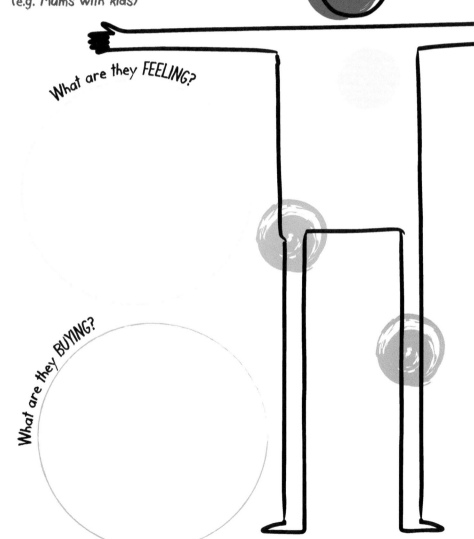

What are they FEELING?

What are they BUYING?

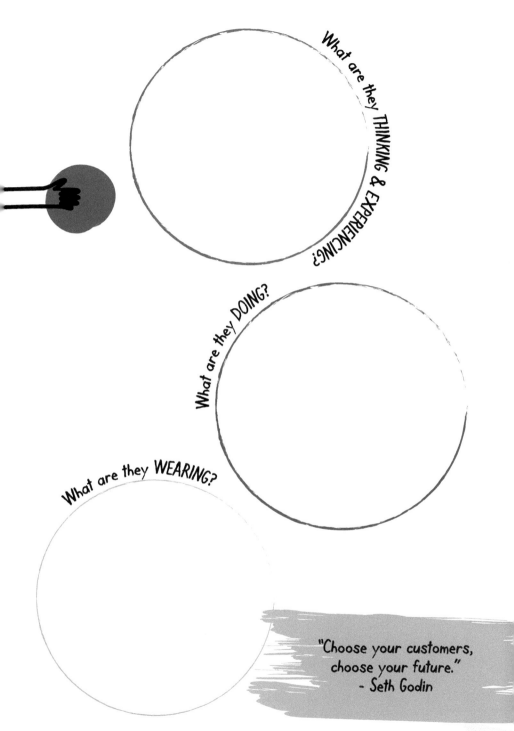

What are they THINKING & EXPERIENCING?

What are they DOING?

What are they WEARING?

"Choose your customers,
choose your future."
- Seth Godin

CUSTOMER PROFILE 2

NAME OF CUSTOMER PROFILE:

What are they FEELING?

What are they BUYING?

What are they WEARING?

"Spend a lot of time talking to customers face to face. You'd be amazed how many companies don't listen to their customer."
- Ross Perot

Think about your customer...

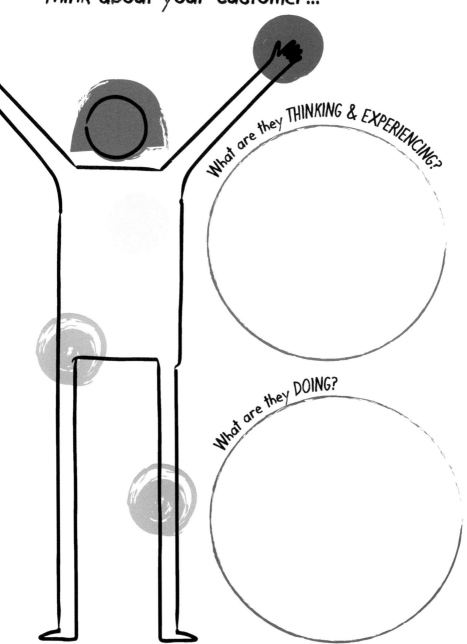

What are they THINKING & EXPERIENCING?

What are they DOING?

CUSTOMER PROFILE 3

NAME OF CUSTOMER PROFILE:

What are they FEELING?

What are they WEARING?

What are they THINKING & EXPERIENCING?

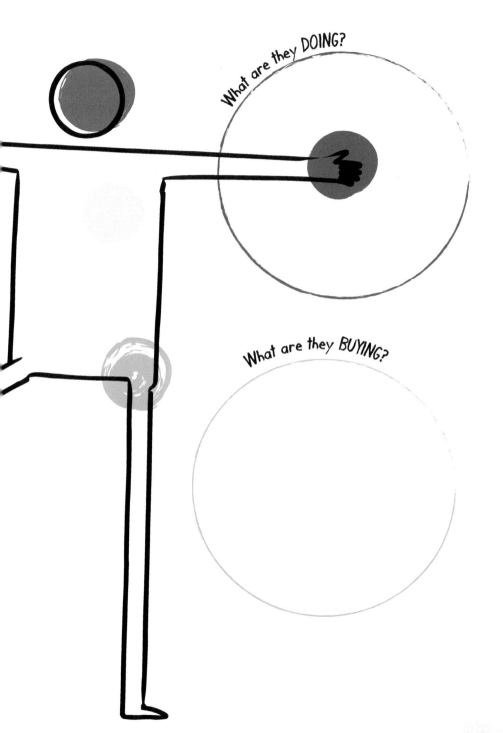

What are they DOING?

What are they BUYING?

NAME OF CUSTOMER PROFILE:

What are they FEELING?

What are they WEARING?

"The aim of marketing is to know and understand the customer so well the product or service fits him and sells itself."
- Peter Drucker

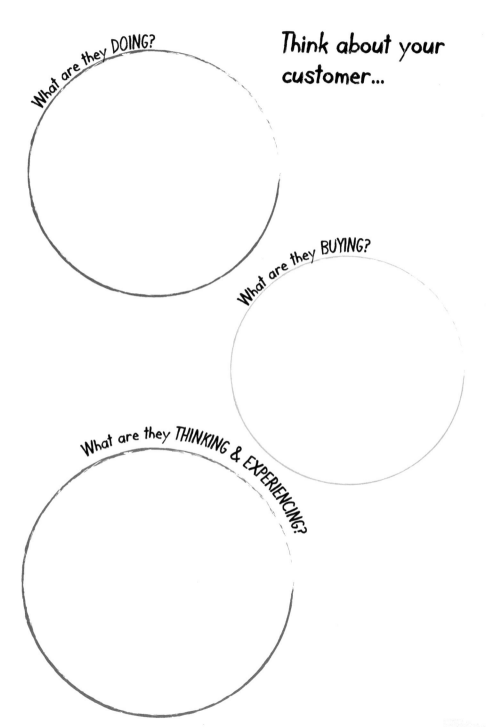

What are they DOING?

Think about your customer...

What are they BUYING?

What are they THINKING & EXPERIENCING?

KNOW YOUR COMPETITION

What do they OFFER?

Think about and research other businesses who offer something similar to you. Record whatever you discover here...

What do they OFFER?

What do they OFFER?

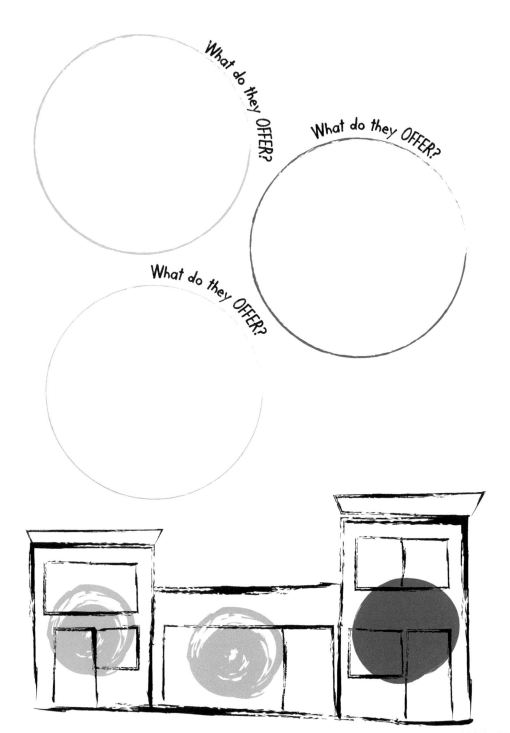

What do they OFFER?

What do they OFFER?

What do they OFFER?

55

Use the space to record the most suitable way you could sell your product or service in each geographical sphere.

(e.g. Local: promotional posters)

(e.g. National: website)

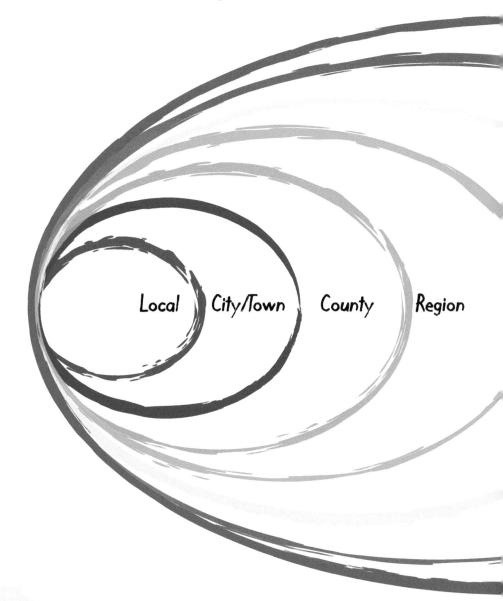

Local   City/Town   County   Region

300

Times the founder of Pandora.com approached investors before he got funding.

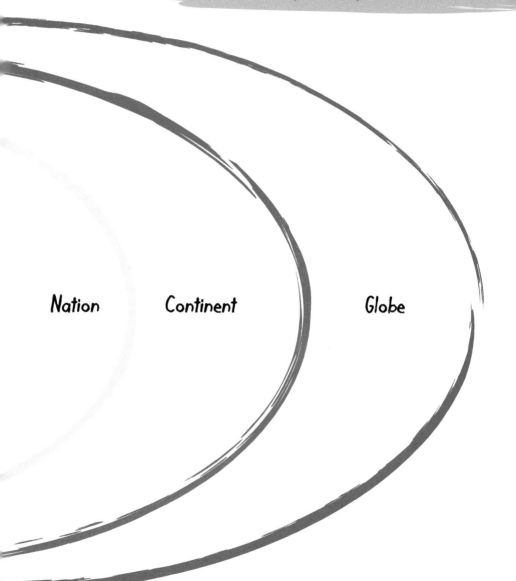

Nation   Continent   Globe

Hit the target with your message...

3. TARGET

Jamal Edwards

"The biggest thing I have learned is not to be scared of failure."

Jamal Edwards was just 15 years old when he turned his hobby into an enterprise in 2006. His parents gave him a video camera as a 15th birthday present and he began recording friends singing and rapping. He launched his YouTube channel, SBTV (the SB comes from his rapping name SmokeyBarz).

Edwards' videos of mostly grime artists such as Dizzie Rascal and Wiley, and later, the singer-songwriter Ed Sheeran, quickly found an enthusiastic audience. With hundreds of thousands of hits on his YouTube channel, he saw a money-making opportunity. He contacted the video-sharing website to see if he was eligible for a share of advertising revenue. He was turned down three times for a YouTube partnership, but persistence paid off. The fourth time he got it, which is when he started making some money on the side.

This success spurred him on, and though Edwards was still in education at this point and also working in a part-time retail job, he says he knew that once I started recording more I could make more money and leave my job at Topman to focus on it full-time. But it took around five years for SBTV's advertising revenues to be enough to provide him a salary.

Since Edwards' business grew from his keen interest in music, that was enough to keep him motivated. "I always say to people do not start a business to make money, you're not going to make money straight away, start it because you're passionate about it. Then hopefully it will start to make money in the long run."

However, it has not always been easy for Edwards and he says making mistakes and learning along the way is not the end of the world. "The biggest thing I have learned is not to be scared of failure."

This mindset of an entrepreneur has paid off and in 2013 SBTV won private equity backing of an undisclosed sum from Miroma Ventures, in a deal that valued the business at £8m. In return, Miroma took a minority stake. As well as all this success Jamal Edwards has also awarded an MBE (Member of the Most Excellent Order of the British Empire) for his services to music.

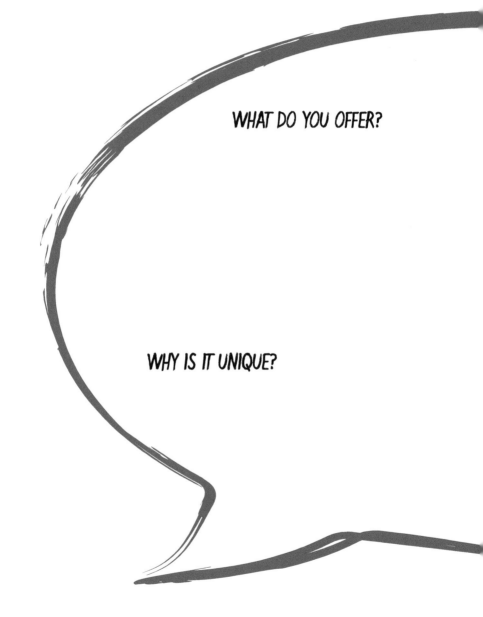

SIMPLE BUSINESS
STORY

WHAT DO YOU OFFER?

WHY IS IT UNIQUE?

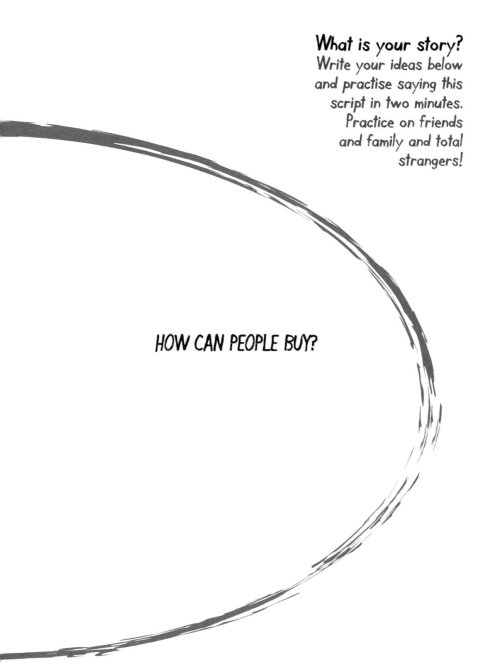

What is your story?
Write your ideas below
and practise saying this
script in two minutes.
Practice on friends
and family and total
strangers!

HOW CAN PEOPLE BUY?

People I will tell this story to in the next two days are...

Write in the images below...

What are your top 3 offers to your customers?

What are the key features of this offer?

OFFER 1:

FEATURES:

OFFER 2:

FEATURES:

OFFER 3:

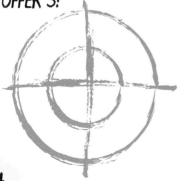

FEATURES:

What are the benefits to your customer of this offer?

BENEFITS:

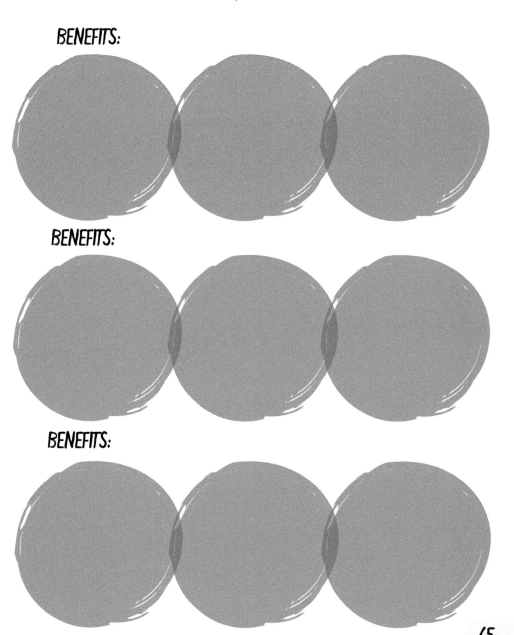

BENEFITS:

BENEFITS:

OBJECTIONS TO SALE

What could your potential customers objections to sales be? (e.g. Cost?)

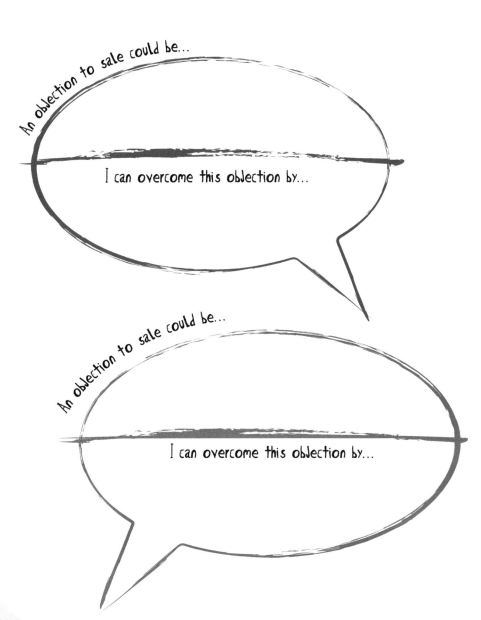

An objection to sale could be...

I can overcome this objection by...

An objection to sale could be...

I can overcome this objection by...

An objection to sale could be...

I can overcome this objection by...

An objection to sale could be...

I can overcome this objection by...

An objection to sale could be...

I can overcome this objection by...

CREATIVE COMMUNICATION

How could you creatively communicate and present your business to an audience?

Draw or write your presentation outline here.

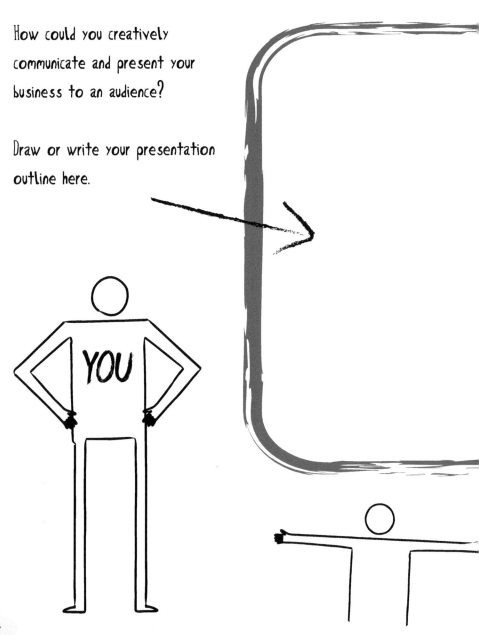

"Passion is the most important element of communication. It is passion, above all, that persuades." - Anita Roddick

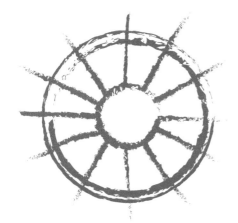

Turn problems into profit and create value...

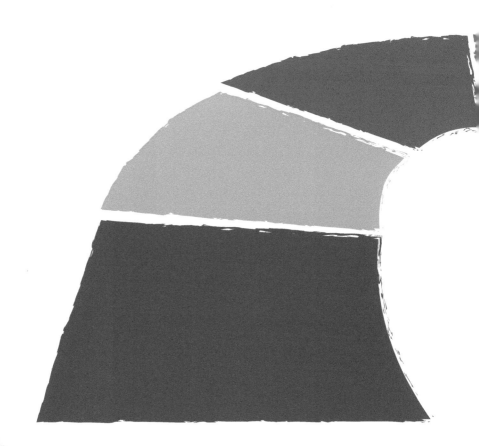

4. WHEEL

Thomas Edison

Thomas Edison was a very patient and passionate man, motivated by success.

Thomas Edison was a very poorly child. Sick lot of his early life, he suffered from a severe ear infection that caused him to be deaf in one of his ears although it has been said he was deaf in both. He also developed scarlet fever as a boy nearly dying because of it, but this didn't stop him achieving.

After becoming a minor celebrity for saving a toddler from being hit by a train, Thomas was offered a job as a telegraph operator.

Thomas went on to create thousands of inventions, holding the patents for 1,093 inventions, however he failed many more times than he succeeded. His first taste of glory came when he developed the tin foil phonograph.

After working as a telegraph operator he wanted to create a way of making a telegraph transmitter to work in a more efficient way. He did this by realising that it sounded very similar to spoken words when the tape from the machine was played at a fast pace. Developing his idea further he went on to record a message through this means, creating his first successful invention that led the way for many more.

Thomas Edison was a very patient and passionate man, motivated by success. He went on to try and failed thousands of times before getting some of his inventions to work. We still use some of his inventions today, and many of them have changed the way we all live, such as the phonograph, the motion picture camera, and the incandescent light bulb.

Notes:

IMPACT

How does your product or
service contribute to the
happiness of your customers?
Write in the wheel...

1500

TIMES SYLVESTER STALLONE WAS REJECTED WHEN HE TRIED SELLING HIS SCRIPT FOR ROCKY

"Customers will want to talk to you if they believe you can solve their problems."
- Jeffery Gitomer

What resources do you already have to hand to create your product/service?

(Use the space in the wheels to write it down)

"Start where you are.
Use what you have.
Do what you can."
- Arthur Ashe

What resources do you need?

PUTTING IT ALL TOGETHER

List the items/services you will need to be able
to make and deliver your product or service...

Item/Service (write in circle)	3 Quotes/Prices from suppliers	Where I will go to get it from (write in house)

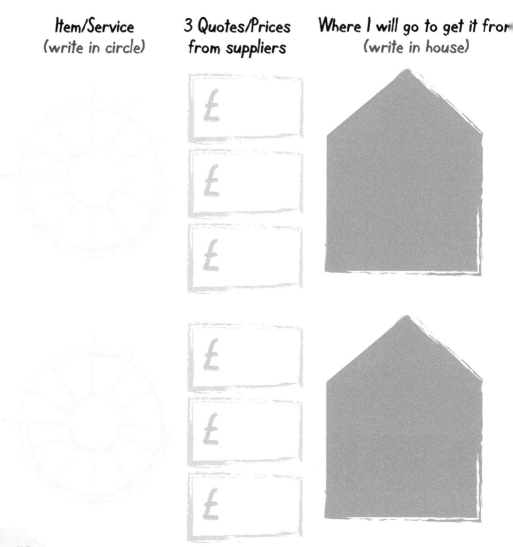

Find and activate your key clients...

5. KEY

Colonel Sanders

Colonel Sanders left Kentucky and travelled to different states to sell his idea, and he kept going until someone said yes!

At 65 years of age Colonel Sanders received his first social security cheque of $99. He was penniless, owned a small house and a run down car. He made a decision that things had to change. His friends used to like his chicken recipe very much. As this was the only novel idea he had, he decided to act upon it.

He left Kentucky and started his travels to different states in the USA to sell his idea. He would tell restaurant owners that he had a chicken recipe which people liked and he was ready to give it to them for free in return for a small percentage on the items sold.

He got rejection after rejection but did not give up, in fact, he got over 1000 rejections. He got 1009 'No's before he got his first 'Yes'. With that one success Colonel Hartland Sanders changed the eating habits of millions of people with Kentucky Fried Chicken, popularly known as KFC.

CONNECTING CUSTOMERS

How can you help your message spread on social media? What ideas do you have for campaigns or ways people can spread your message?

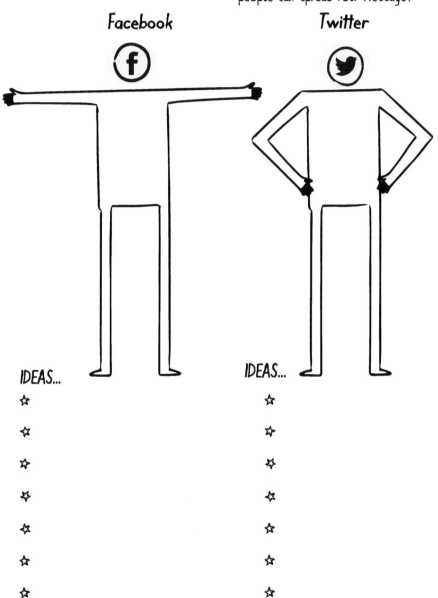

Facebook

Twitter

IDEAS...
☆
☆
☆
☆
☆
☆
☆

IDEAS...
☆
☆
☆
☆
☆
☆
☆

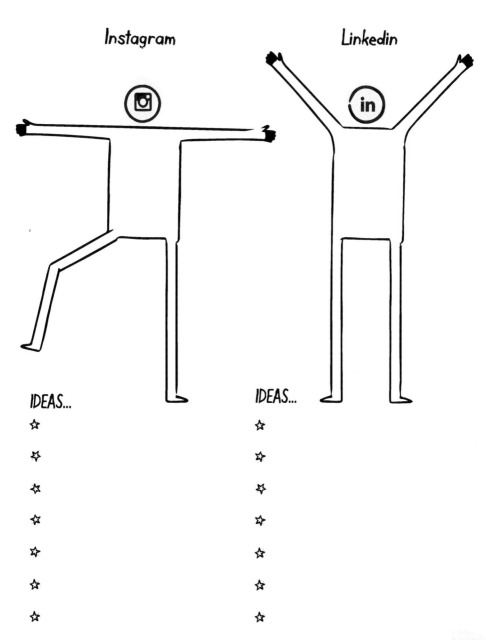

Instagram

Linkedin

IDEAS...
☆
☆
☆
☆
☆
☆
☆

IDEAS...
☆
☆
☆
☆
☆
☆
☆

TRAFFIC LIGHTS

Are you moving your customers from red to green?
Use the following pages to assess your customers...

"STOP"
Who do you still need to "STOP" and sell to?

"GET READY"
Who is interested in what you are offering but haven't commited to buy yet?

"GO"
Who are your customers that you need to activate to become repeat clients, to refer people to you and recommend you to others?

"Loyal customers, they don't just come back, they don't simply recommend you, they insist that their friends do business with you." - Chip Bell

CUSTOMERS TO STOP

Do you have any customers you know need to be "stopped"?
(e.g. people who haven't heard about your product/service yet?)

Use the space in the traffic light to write notes...

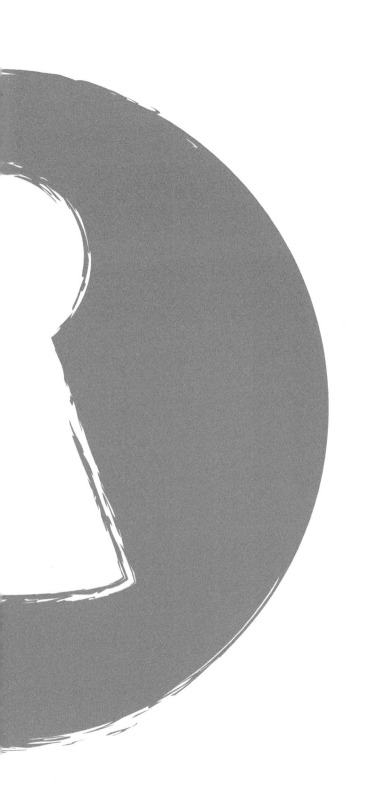

CUSTOMERS TO GET READY

Who has heard about
your business but has not
committed to buy yet?

What do you need to do
next with them?
(How will you "get them
ready" to buy?)

Use the space in the
traffic light to write
notes...

Do you have any customers who now need to be activated to "go" and spread the message to all their contacts?

How can you help them do that?

Use the space in the traffic light to write notes...

5126

Times James Dyson created prototypes that failed before he succeeded to move air at 400mph

"A good reputation is more valuable than money."
- Publius Syrus

What are your Top 3 offers?
What is the cost of producing them, their value and the price you will charge your clients?

Name of offer: Cost:

1    £

2   £

3   £

COST – the amount you spend producing your product/service
VALUE – what you believe your product/service is worth
PRICE – the amount you will charge your customer

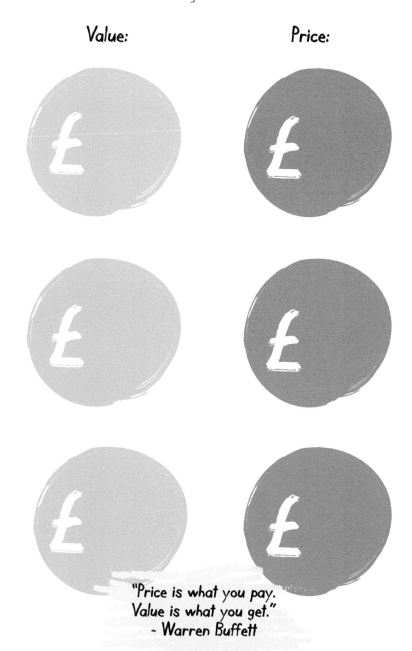

Value: Price:

"Price is what you pay.
Value is what you get."
- Warren Buffett

PRICE COMPARISON

Compare your prices
with your competitors...

**Name of my
Product/Service**

Our Price

What is the difference between their offering and price and yours? (Write in the circles...)

Name of competitor
and their price

What's the difference?

Help your customers have an excellent experience!

6. PLAY

Rita Sharma

'It went from boom to bust, almost... I was selling business class tickets I had to quickly learn to sell to people who were travelling economy.'

Rita Sharma founded the travel agency 'Worldwide Journey' in 1986 as a bespoke travel agency. It was rebranded to 'Best At Travel' in 2003 and has since expanded to provide other services including cruises and flights and reported a turnover of £81 million and gross profit of £8.4 million in December 31, 2014.

Born in India but brought up in Ilford, Essex, since childhood, Rita dropped out of law school at Sussex University after a term to start her travel agency. Her husband, Rahul Sharma is an accountant who joined the business shortly after its formation. Rita was awarded an OBE (Officer of the Most Excellent Order of the British Empire) in 2007.

"The first office was the size of a broom cupboard" she says. "It was really small, and we had no windows or anything. All I had was two desks and some phones." Her business was focused initially on selling transatlantic business flights but in 1987 or 88, when the stock market crashed, so did the business. "It went from boom to bust, almost. It all happened in one year. People were no longer spending ridiculous amounts of money travelling first or club class. Because I was selling business class tickets I had to quickly learn to sell to people who were travelling economy."

Fortunately leisure travel became a growth area and Worldwide Journeys began to carve out a profitable niche in bespoke holiday packages.

"We are not in the business of selling a bit of this, a bit of that, flights and hotels. We sell the entire dream, a bespoke tailor-made holiday, from the flights to the hotel to the transfers and the tour the whole thing. And we sell very high-end, luxury travel."

CUSTOMER EXPERIENCE

What do you want your customers experience to be?

What do you want them to see?

What do you want them to feel?

"A satisfied customer is the best business strategy of all."
- Michael LeBoeuf

What do you want them to be saying?

What do you want them to hear?

What do you want them to taste?

What feedback do you want from your customers and why?

YOU

How will you get this information?

Customer

What will you do with this information?

10,000
Times Thomas Edison created failed prototypes of his electric bulb before succeeding.

BUILD YOUR TEAM

Do you need a team?
What will their roles be?
What responsibilities will they have?
Who could it be?

Role?

Responsibilities?

Who?

Role?

Responsibilities?

Who?

Role?

Responsibilities?

Who?

Role?

Responsibilities?

Who?

Role?

Responsibilities?

Who?

6 QUESTION ACTION PLAN

WHAT NEEDS TO BE DONE?	WHY?	HOW?

Use this template action plan to organise yourself!

WHERE?	WHO?	WHEN?

Get the basics in place...

Money matters & legal stuff!

7. MULTIPLY

Pip Murray

'There are lots of alternative means to get your business up and running ... it just takes a bit more creative thinking.'

By the age of 28, Pip Murray has established an award-winning nutritious nut butter range with no palm oils or refined sugars which is stocked in Selfridges, Ocado, Wholefoods, Sainsburys and over 2,000 other big name stores. Having started her enterprise from a garden shed in 2013 after gaining inspiration from her love of marathon running, Murray claims to be on set to achieve start-up revenues of £3.3m by the end of 2016.

In 2015, the entrepreneur was recognised by Sir Richard Branson as having created one of Britain's "hottest new food businesses" and won the chance to pitch to buyers at the Target Corporation in the US. Backed by £200,000 in private and equity crowdfunding, Murray is now looking to scale Pip & Nut with European expansion on the cards.

She says "Moving into a shed might seem like a bit of an unusual, and drastic step to take to launch a business but for me it gave me just the leg up that I needed to get my business, Pip & Nut, off the ground... It's been just over a year in the planning and like a lot of start-ups it's certainly been a challenging year with several hurdles to jump in order to get my product to market. But in the last couple of months the major blocks that I'd been facing tended to boil down to two main factors. Time and money.

"I won a competition run by Escape the City, a company who help talented individuals leave their unfulfilling corporate day jobs. The Escape the City founders decided to run the 'Escape to the Shed' competition after their own experience of needing to quit their day jobs, to give their company more time to grow, but at the same time still being reliant on their jobs to pay their London rent."

The 'Escape to the Shed' competition was an opportunity for them to help another start-up out by giving them three months free rent in the shed in central London and desk space.

"I was short-listed to compete in a Facebook competition, alongside 12 other start-up companies, and after lobbying as hard as I could for two weeks to get as many 'likes' on the Pip & Nut page my business was announced as the winner."

"Since winning Pip & Nut has moved forwards in leaps and bounds. It meant I could afford to quit my job, which I did just an hour after finding out I'd won, and go full-time on the business – enabling me to give it the time it fundamentally needed."

"This competition is a classic example of how help comes in all sorts of guises. There are lots of alternative means to get your business up and running before looking for larger financial backing, it just takes a bit more creative thinking."

NOTES

SURVIVAL BUDGET

How much money do you need to survive?

EXPENDITURE	MONTHLY COST	YEARLY COST
MORTGAGE AND/OR RENT		
COUNCIL TAX		
UTILITIES (GAS, ELECTRICITY, WATER ETC.)		
PHONE AND INTERNET		
CAR TAX AND INSURANCE		
CAR RUNNING EXPENSES		
HP REPAYMENTS		
HIRE CHARGES		
SUBSCRIPTIONS TO JOURNALS, PROFESSIONAL BODIES ETC.		
SAVING PLANS AND PENSION CONTRIBUTIONS		
CONTINGENCIES		
TAX		
NATIONAL INSURANCE		
OTHER		
OTHER		
OTHER		
OTHER		
OTHER		
	TOTAL: £	TOTAL: £

MONEY SPENT

keep a record of your spending...

DATE OF PURCHASE (DD/MM/YYYY)	ITEM PURCHASED AND REASON	UNIT COST (£)
01/10/2017	Cake decorations	0.20

QUANTITY	AMOUNT SPENT (£)	CASH OR INVOICE	DATE PAID (DD/MM/YYYY)	RECEIPTS FILED (YES OR NO)
24	4.80	Cash	01/10/2017	Yes

keep a record of your income!

DATE OF RECEIVED (DD/MM/YYYY)	RECEIVED FROM AND REASON
01/10/2017	Cash from customer - paid in advance for cake

AMOUNT RECEIVED (£)	PAPERWORK FILED (WRITE YES OR NO WHEN COMPLETED)
20	YES

COST OF YOUR BUSINESS

Below is a table to help you identify the cost of starting up your business.

CATEGORY	ITEM	FREQUENCY	COST (£)
PRODUCT/SERVICE			
			TOTAL
MARKETING			
			TOTAL
			TOTAL
TRAVEL			
			TOTAL
OTHER			
			TOTAL
			GRAND TOTAL

INVESTMENT

What investment do you need to start-up your enterprise?
(Write in the circles...)

What do you need this investment for?

When do we need it?

From who/where will you get it?

How will you get it?

OBSTACLES

What obstacles and challenges will you face on the start-up path?

What challenges?

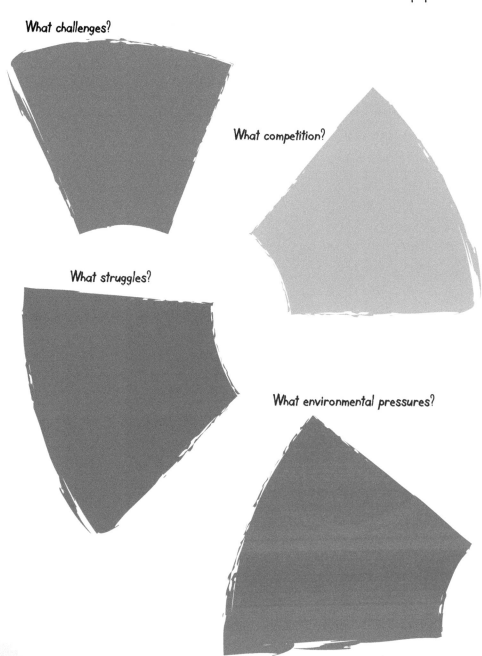

What competition?

What struggles?

What environmental pressures?

What circumstances?

What relationship challenges?

What financial setbacks?

"Our greatest weakness lies in giving up.
The most certain way to succeed is always to try
just one more time." - Thomas Edison

What have been the joys and challenges of your steps on the path so far?

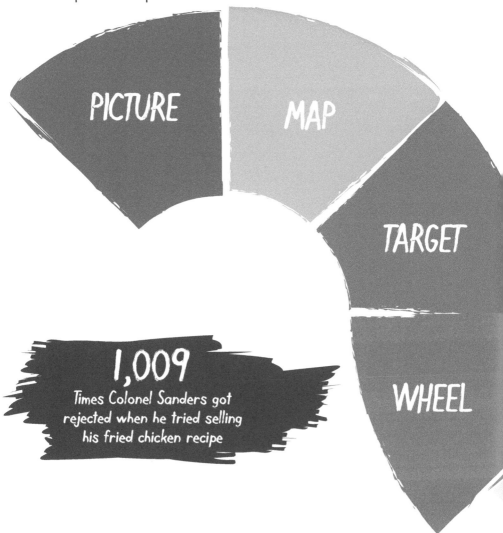

PICTURE

MAP

TARGET

WHEEL

1,009
Times Colonel Sanders got rejected when he tried selling his fried chicken recipe

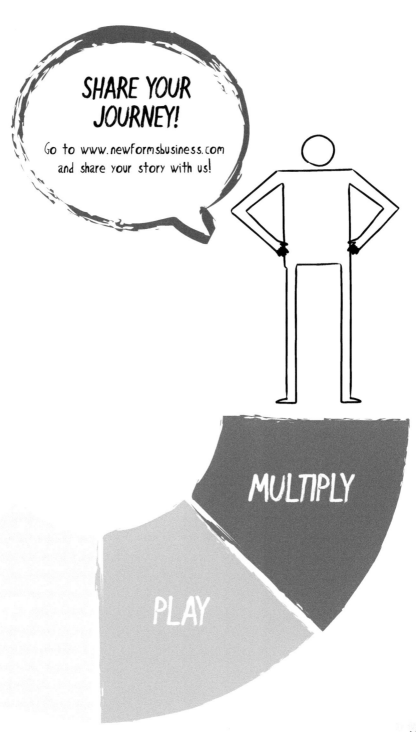

YOUR BUSINESS

NOW IT'S TIME TO BUILD!

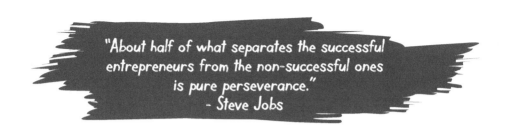

"About half of what separates the successful entrepreneurs from the non-successful ones is pure perseverance."
- Steve Jobs

Visit www.newformsbusiness.com to take it to the next level!

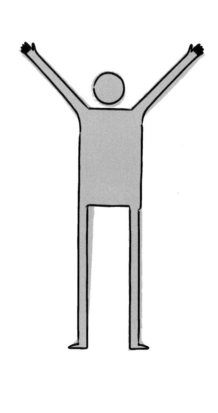

About the author: Peter J Farmer

Peter is a coach, trainer and mentor. He has a particular interest in movements and connecting with people globally. He travels extensively across the British Isles and Europe, speaking, mentoring and training. Peter is a consumer of culture, future trends spotter and lover of music. He founded Newforms.

newforms

Newforms is a collaborative incubator of creativity and innovation, seeking to facilitate change across all spheres of society, using games as a powerful tool to achieve this. Whether you are starting up in enterprise, growing your business, or expanding your vision to multiply your brand, Newforms has innovative training packages for all. There are three levels of training available; the BusinessPath for pre-start and start-ups, the BusinessHouse for business growth and the BusinessLandscape for expansion.

BusinessPath

Are you ready to launch your business idea? Our 'BusinessPath' workshops cover the main themes of the Start-Up journey introduced in this BusinessPath Journal. These workshops will support and equip you to continue your journey from initial idea to launch and help you pick up the vital enterprise skills needed for your venture to succeed!

BusinessHouse

Are you ready to to grow your business to the next level? Playing the BusinessHouse as part of these workshops will activate vital skills for leadership & management, development and business growth. The BusinessHouse helps you grow your business into a fully developed, growing business – a 'full house' of teams and profitable activity! As a result of the training, you will develop a growth plan and gain the skills and confidence in Strategy, Innovation, Marketing, Managing and Operations.

BusinessLandscape

Are you wanting to expand your vision and multiply your brand across new horizons? The BusinessLandscape training workshops will equip you to do this as you discover and fill new places, people groups and social spheres with your brand, developing the infrastructure needed along the way.

To find out more and experience Newforms Training go to www.newformsbusiness.com